31.00

GRAPHIC PREHISTORIC ANIMALS

TERMINATOR PIG

DAEODON

ILLUSTRATED BY ALESSANDRO POLUZZI

A+

Smart Apple Media

Published by Smart Apple Media, an imprint of Black Rabbit Books
P.O. Box 3263, Mankato, Minnesota 56002
www.blackrabbitbooks.com

Produced by David West ☂ Children's Books
6 Princeton Court, 55 Felsham Road, London SW15 1AZ

Designed and written by Gary Jeffrey

Cataloging-in-Publication data is on file with the Library of Congress.
ISBN 978-1-62588-412-1
eBook ISBN 978-1-62588-428-2

Printed in China
CPSIA compliance information: DWCB16CP
010116

9 8 7 6 5 4 3 2 1

CONTENTS

WHAT IS A TERMINATOR PIG?

ENTELODONT MEANS "PERFECT TOOTH"

The piglike enteledont *Daeodon* lived around 29 million to 19 million years ago, during the late **Oligocene** to early **Miocene periods. Fossils** of its skeleton have been found in North America (see page 22).

Its head was 3 feet (91 cm) long.

It had bony lumps sticking out from its cheeks much like a modern-day warthog.

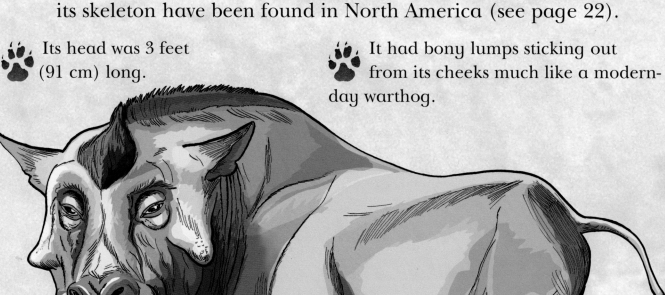

Its brain was the size of an orange, so it wasn't very smart.

It was an omnivore, which means it fed on both meat and plants.

DAEODON (DREADFUL TEETH) MEASURED UP TO 11 FEET (3.4 M) LONG, 8 FEET (2.4 M) HIGH, AND WEIGHED 930 POUNDS (420 KG).

It was more like a hippopotamus than a true pig.

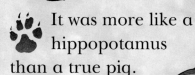

This would be *Daeodon* and you.

ANIMAL FACTS

Archaeotherium *was the first big entelodont.*

In contrast to the warthog, entelodonts' eyes faced forward, so they could judge the distance to prey. This, and their fearsome-looking teeth, have caused some scientists to label them top hunters. Others disagree, saying their lack of claws would have prevented them from bringing down running prey. What is known is that they would grub around for roots.

The first entelodonts were the size of modern wild pigs. Seven kinds have been discovered, each getting larger than the one before. Entelodonts looked a lot like modern-day warthogs—especially their bony cheek **nodules**. Male warthogs use these to scare off rivals. Scientists think entelodonts may have done the same. Their probable aggression, size, and teeth would have made entelodonts a tough rival for other **predators** to compete with.

The latest and largest entelodont was *Daeodon*. This super-size terminator pig rose to the top of the food chain in North America. Back then, the area was like today's Serengeti in East Africa.

TERMINATOR PIG ON THE MIDWEST AMERICAN PLAINS

THE PLAINS OF WHAT IS NOW NEBRASKA, 19 MILLION YEARS AGO.

A GROUP OF MOROPUS CHALICOTHERES LUMBER OUT OF THE TREES THAT EDGE THE BANKS OF A SHALLOW RIVER. IT IS THE MIDDLE OF THE DRY SEASON, AND THE MOROPUSES HAVE TAKEN A BREAK FROM THEIR ALMOST CONSTANT LEAF MUNCHING TO DRINK.

BOUAARGH

NERVOUS MERYCHIPPUS HORSES AND STENOMYLUS CAMELS SCATTER, LEAVING A PATH TO THE WATER'S EDGE CLEAR.

THE OLDEST MOROPUS IS STRUGGLING IN THE HEAT AND IS SOME WAY BEHIND.

IT HAS BEEN SEEN BY ANOTHER ANIMAL THAT IS STANDING QUIETLY IN THE SHADE OF THE TREES.

IT IS SHARP-EYED AND WAITS PATIENTLY FOR ITS MOMENT.

THE OLD MOROPUS STUMBLES, ITS HEAD DROOPING, AND GIVES OUT A DRY, WHEEZING CALL. THE COOLING WATER SUDDENLY SEEMS A LONG DISTANCE AWAY.

HUFF HUFF

GWHEEEEEE...

THE HUMP-BACKED ANIMAL LUNGES FORWARD, BREAKING COVER. IT IS A FULL-GROWN DAEODON—A TERMINATOR PIG.

THE DAEODON TROTS TOWARD THE FALLEN MOROPUS. IT HAS TO BE CAREFUL OF THE ANIMAL'S LONG ARMS AND CLAWED HANDS.

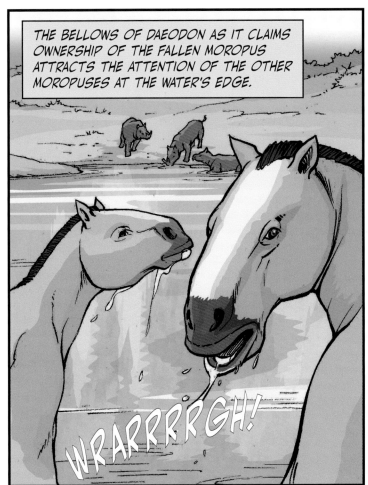

THE BELLOWS OF DAEODON AS IT CLAIMS OWNERSHIP OF THE FALLEN MOROPUS ATTRACTS THE ATTENTION OF THE OTHER MOROPUSES AT THE WATER'S EDGE.

WRARRRRGH!

TWO OF THEM LUMBER BACK TOWARD THE FALLEN ELDER.

BY NOW THE DAEODON HAS DUG ITS FRONT TEETH DEEP INTO THE MOROPUS' SHOULDER.

BRAAAAARE!   GWHEEEEEEEEEE

A MATURE MALE MOROPUS LEANS TOWARD THE DAEODON, STAMPING ITS CLAWS DOWN HARD ON THE EARTH. ITS COMPANION MOVES IN TO SHIELD THE HELPLESS OLD ONE.

DESPITE ITS SIZE, THE DAEODON FEELS OUTNUMBERED AND BACKS OFF TOWARD THE SCRUB.

BUT IT STAYS CLOSE BY. IT CAN WAIT.

IT IS NOW ONLY A MATTER OF TIME.

DWARF VULTURES WHEEL IN SPIRALLING **THERMALS**. IT IS TWO HOURS SINCE THE ATTACK AND THE OLD MOROPUS HAS DIED FROM BLOOD LOSS AND SHOCK.

ITS COMPANIONS LEAVE IT AND MOVE AWAY IN SEARCH OF FOOD.

AS VULTURES LAND NEARBY, THE DROOLING DAEODON TROTS FORWARD TO THE FRESH CARCASS.

INSIDE DAEODON'S MOUTH ARE ALL THE TOOLS IT NEEDS. FORWARD **INCISORS** TEAR OFF GREAT CHUNKS OF MEAT.

SHARP **MOLAR** SIDE TEETH SLICE AND CHEW FLESH.

MASSIVE FANGED **CANINES** HELP CRUSH AND SPLIT BONE, RELEASING THE **NUTRITIOUS** MARROW INSIDE IT.

AS DAEODON **GORGES**, THE KILL ATTRACTS SMALLER SCAVENGERS, SUCH AS CARRION CROWS AND DOGLIKE BOROPHAGUSES. THEY GATHER NEARBY, READY TO FIGHT OVER WHATEVER THE ENTELODONT LEAVES.

MONTHS GO BY AND STILL THERE IS NO RAINFALL. THE STRIP OF RIVER IN THE DAEODON'S TERRITORY HAS SHRUNK TO A SHALLOW, MUDDY POOL.

THE FAST AND AGILE GRAZERS, SUCH AS HORSES AND CAMELS, LEFT THE AREA LONG AGO. ONLY MENOCERAUSES REMAIN. THEY WALLOW IN THE FAST-DRYING MUD, BUT THERE IS LITTLE LEFT TO EAT.

THE DAEODON HAS GROWN FAT FEEDING ON THE MANY WEARY ANIMALS THAT HAVE TRUDGED TO THE WATERHOLE AND DIED THERE.

A PACK OF FIVE BEARDOGS TROT DOWN FROM THE HIGH GROUND. THE THREE **JUVENILES** AND ONE **YEARLING** ARE LED BY A SOLITARY MALE. THE LONG DROUGHT AND THE LACK OF PREY HAVE FORCED THE BEARDOGS TO EXTEND THEIR TERRITORY...

...WHICH NOW INCLUDES THE DAEODON'S POOL.

THE BONES OF THE EATEN ANIMALS, SHATTERED AND STRIPPED OF MARROW, LITTER THE MUDHOLE WHERE THE LAST OF THE MENOCERAUSES LIE DEAD IN THE MIDDAY SUN.

OVERHEATED AND PANTING HEAVILY, THE DAEODON PICKS ITS WAY TO THE CENTER.

WHEN THIS CARRION IS GONE, THE ENTELODONT WILL BE FORCED TO USE ITS FANGS TO GRUB FOR ROOTS AND TUBERS UNTIL THE RAINS COME.

VULTURES HAVE ALREADY BEGUN TO PICK AT THE MENOCERAUSES' SKIN, TEARING HOLES, WHICH LET OUT A SICKLY SWEET STENCH.

THE DAEODON RUSHES FORWARD AND GROWLS TO SCARE OFF THE BIRDS AND CLAIM THE CARCASSES.

RRRRAAGH!

BUT IT IS NOT ALONE.

A JUVENILE BEARDOG AT THE EDGE OF THE POOL SNIFFS THE AIR AND BELLOWS LOUDLY TO SUMMON THE PACK.

WRAAAARRR!

THEY ARRIVE AND FAN OUT TOWARD THE FEEDING DAEODON, BARKING AND YELPING TO EACH OTHER IN EXCITEMENT.

YOWL

WAROOOU

WUFF

YIP-YIP

THE LEADER AND THREE JUVENILES CIRCLE AROUND THE ENTELODONT. IT TURNS TO FACE THEM AND GROWLS ANGRILY.

HUNGER OVERCOMES THE YEARLING'S NATURAL CAUTION AS IT EDGES ITS WAY FORWARD TO STEAL A PIECE OF MEAT.

THE DAEODON TURNS ON IT, SNARLING. THE SOUND IS A WARNING. AS THE YEARLING DARTS BACKWARD WITH ITS PRIZE, THE BATTLE BEGINS.

THE BEARDOG PACK TAKE TURNS SNATCHING BITES OF THE CARCASSES, MAKING THE DAEODON SPIN THIS WAY AND THAT AS IT TRIES TO STOP THEM.

AS THE BIG ENTELODONT TIRES, THE BEARDOGS GROW BOLDER. THEY FORM A UNITED, SNARLING LINE AND DRIVE THE DAEODON FROM ITS MEAL.

UNWILLING TO GIVE UP, THE DAEODON TURNS AND CHARGES AT THE BEARDOGS.

ITS TINY BRAIN IS NO MATCH FOR THEIR CUNNING. ALL IT HAS IS SPEED, SIZE, AND DETERMINED AGGRESSION.

IT PILES INTO THE BEARDOGS, SWINGING ITS MASSIVE HEAD FROM SIDE TO SIDE. IT SCATTERS THEM AND NARROWLY MISSES THE PACK LEADER.

THE YEARLING IS NOT SO LUCKY. IT GETS SWIPED IN THE HEAD BY ONE OF THE DAEODON'S TUSKS.

THE DAEODON REACTS SPEEDILY AND BITES THE DAZED BEARDOG ON THE HEAD BEFORE IT CAN MOVE.

CLUMP!

THE DAEODON EYES THE PACK. SURELY IT HAS WON THE CONTEST.

BUT THE BEARDOGS WILL NOT GIVE UP. ONE OF THE JUVENILES LUNGES FORWARD AND LOCKS ON TO THE DAEODON'S TAIL.

THE PACK LEADER JUMPS IN AND BITES FIRMLY INTO THE DAEODON'S THIGH. THE JUVENILE TUGS HARD AT ITS TAIL, NOT LETTING GO.

IT'S TOO MUCH. THE BEARDOG PACK FINALLY DRIVES THE DAEODON AWAY FROM THE FEAST FOR GOOD.

SORE AND TIRED, THE DAEODON LIMPS AWAY WITH THE BEARDOG IT CAUGHT. BUT THE BEARDOGS' TEAMWORK HAS WON AGAINST THE DAEODON'S SIZE AND STRENGTH.

THE TIME OF THE TERMINATOR PIGS IS DRAWING TO A CLOSE.

FOSSIL FINDS

WE CAN GET A GOOD IDEA OF WHAT **ANCIENT ANIMALS** MAY HAVE LOOKED LIKE FROM THEIR FOSSILS. FOSSILS ARE FORMED WHEN THE HARD PARTS OF AN ANIMAL OR PLANT BECOME BURIED AND THEN TURN TO ROCK OVER MILLIONS OF YEARS.

In the spreading grasslands of the early Miocene, prey animals, such as horses and camels, evolved to run faster, which made them harder to catch. This caused the end of the large, hyena-like animals that had been the entelodont's main rivals. The climate's change to dry seasons and extended droughts meant there were plentiful carcasses, which entelodonts, such as *Daeodon*, were able to scavenge and feed on.

Entelodonts grew bigger but not smarter in the evolutionary race.

Hundreds of fossilized rhinoceroses were found at Agate Springs in Nebraska, in what was once a shallow riverbed, along with two *Daeodons* and some beardogs. *Daeodons* disappear from the fossil record as beardogs turn up. These more intelligent hunters edged out the terminator pigs by ganging up to steal their kills. They also ran down larger game by working as a team, in the way modern wolves do.

22

ANIMAL GALLERY

All of these **animals** appear in the story.

Stenomylus
"narrow molar"
height: 2 ft (61 cm)
a tiny camel with the build of a
modern gazelle that probably
roamed in large herds

Menoceras
"crescent horns"
length: 5 ft (1.5 m)
a rhinoceros the size of a large
pig; males had two small side-
by-side nose horns

Merychippus
"ruminant horse"
height: 3 ft (91 cm)
a three-toed grazing horse
that thrived in herds on the
Miocene grasslands

Borophagus
"gluttonous eater"
length: 2.6 ft (79 cm)
a heavy-set, coyote-sized dog with a bulging
forehead and bone-crushing jaws, similar to a
modern-day hyena

Dwarf vulture
Hadrogyps aigialeus
length: 2 ft (61 cm)
a condorlike vulture—one of the rare birds
found in the North American
Miocene fossil layer

Beardog
Daphoenodon
length: 5-6 ft (1.5–1.8 m)
a strongly-built, catlike dog the size of a small
wolf that had powerful bone-crushing jaws

Moropus
"slow foot"
height at the shoulder: 8 ft (2.4 m)
a horselike leafeater—that had claws instead of
hooves and long forelimbs

GLOSSARY

canine a pointed tooth between the front teeth and cheek teeth of a
  mammal, enlarged for flesh-tearing in meat eaters

carrion rotting flesh of dead animals

fossil the remains of living things that have turned to rock

gorge to stuff one's mouth full of food

incisor a chisel-edged front tooth for biting

juvenile not yet fully grown

Miocene period the time between 23,000,000 to 5,000,000 years ago
  when grasslands slowly replaced Earth's forests

molar a cheek tooth for chewing

nodule a rounded swelling of body cells

Oligocene period the time between 34,000,000 to 23,000,000 years ago
  when great tropical forests reduced

predator an animal that naturally preys on others

thermal a current of hot rising air that aids bird flight

yearling a young animal in its first or second year

INDEX

Liv April 2017

Liv April 2017